D1621925

The Dollhouse Mirror

Poetry by Frank Watson

Edited by Boris Komatina

Plum White Press

Published by Plum White Press LLC

For information concerning reprints, email PlumWhitePress@gmail.com

ISBN-13:	9781939832122
ISBN-10:	1939832128
LCCN:	2014952248
BISAC:	Poetry / General

Cover design by Cornelia G. Murariu, copyright © 2014 by Plum White Press LLC

We would like to acknowledge *Arcana: The Tarot Anthology*, published by Minor Arcana Press, in which "he's a lion" will appear.

Published in the United States of America

Also by Frank Watson

In the Dark, Soft Earth
Seas to Mulberries
One Hundred Leaves

Contact

⭕ 🅵 🆃 @FrankWatsonPoet

frankwatsonpoet@gmail.com

www.frankwatsonpoet.com

The Dollhouse Mirror

Poetry by Frank Watson

to the poet
there is a love of beauty
in all its
terrifying forms

she was a doe
with tender flesh
but the only ones
she loved
were hungry wolves

darkly burning
beneath the raven moon

this frigid night
I wait for you

in the dark waters
of night
she keeps warm
with a fire
that burns in her heart

—The Tarot "Chariot"

lifting your head
to the wind
you welcome the sun
dropped tears
with open eyes

between the lines
he slips
into the warm
darkness of her kiss

sun mixed
within the clouds

I feel the warmth
beneath your veil

the forest
curled up
into a story
of stranded souls
away from city lights

this endless earth
where I have grown
with the weeds
and learned from the birds
to fly away free

raving
through a long
night of desire

when all the madness
has sunk

into a warm
pillow's rest

even on
the darkest night
there are stars
that she can look up to

—The Tarot "Chariot"

her cave is dark
but from within
you can see
the entire cosmos

—The Tarot "High Priestess"

in the forest
of haunted dreams
she closes her eyes
in tranquil sleep

when all eternity is rest
why not use this time
to do my best?

her robe is held
by a simple pin

but no one
will get past the sword

that protects
what's underneath

—The Tarot "Justice"

he's a lion
at her dress
but she tames him
in sweet caress

—The Tarot "Strength"

because
she did not seek
the golden bird

it rested on her branch
in peace

—The Tarot "Empress"

I found you
in a cavern
by the woods
in the howl
of moonlit ecstasy

like golden moons
they bathed in the water
of each other's reflection

she lies there wet
in the soap-stained water
with clothes laid out
for an evening tryst

pausing in that
moment of light
between the steps
of now
and imagination

swimming
in the heartbeat
of her words

I hear the melody
of another life

his soul was bright
like a remnant of light
that quivers in the shade

you sleep
beneath the moon
as I slip
into the covers
of imagination

paths
between
the grass

and the
fragrant harvest
of your
goodnight kiss

a doll stares out
the store window
at the little girl
of her dreams

the spirits have fled
across the sea
and all the gentle voices
have washed ashore

washing my face
a thousand times
the mask remains in place

your voice
in the leaves
and a name
that's carved
into the forest's
weeping wood

we kiss
in silence

our memories
a journey

that ended
not long ago

alone among the flowers
sleeping beneath the sun
our love's a fallen shower
whose water path has run

the raven
guides my feet
on this long night
through the forest
of restless sleep

the little girl's
ribbons and bows
reflect like glass
in the old
woman's soul

why cry
when there is chance

and a path
that will lead you there?

spinning
in that world
of memory
and desire
just out of reach

yesterday she loved him
but now he's too old;
oh, how the little bee
has lost his sting
and now the flower folds

it was
an empty garden
but the scent
of last night's kiss
still lingers
in the morning

between
the day and night
I walk
as a shadow
in the light

flower cut
from the stem
in the beautiful
minute
before its death

suspended
by a branch

this was
the first time
he felt free

—The Tarot "Hanged Man"

painted in dust
he sees the face of fear
with no one to trust
he thrusts his spear

—Unknown Soldier

he holds
a shadow
of the light
they used to
share together

—The Tarot "Temperance"

spinning
the wheel of life
he sees the family
that could have been

there was one
lover too many

in the garden
that would've been
Eden

all the dust
that's swept into
the world's wind
and the particle
that is me

he waits
in the crevice
of earth
to sail out
on a gentler day

he looks around
but the enemy
is within

her skin
is moonlight
on the shores

where I am wrecked
and will not return

pallid and hollow
we've drifted
in this town
for centuries
and no one's home

with a tear
she told herself
that sometimes
a rose is just a rose

he wanted to return
but there was no way back
from where he'd gone

dust in the wind
on the day
we parted our ways

floating in
the midnight smoke
I fade like
the howls of a wolf
on a long, blue night

seed planted
on the grave
of yesterday's tears

he opened
countless doors
but never found a way out
from his inner
torture

she sat
with Humpty Dumpty
and gave him
a little push
(for such is life)

all the real men
have gone
to the sky

she thought
with a gaze
at where he lies

there is time
enough for weeping
as the dust settles
and all the books
remain closed

.

Made in the USA
Columbia, SC
02 March 2021